INTO THE EARLY HOURS

INTO

the

EARLY

HOURS

Lynn,

I was a fan

Aislinn Hunter

before you gave me

street cred.

xo (Thanks.)

POLESTAR
An Imprint of Raincoast Books

Aislinn

Vancity Oct 2007

Polestar Books and Raincoast Books gratefully acknowledge the support of the Government of Canada
through the Book Publishing Industry Development Program, the Canada Council and the Department
of Canadian Heritage. We also acknowledge the assistance of the Province of British Columbia through
the British Columbia Arts Council.

Edited by Lynn Henry
Design by Val Speidel
Cover photograph by Steve Ibb/Photonica
Author photograph by Glenn Hunter

National Library of Canada Cataloguing in Publication Data

Hunter, Aislinn, 1969–
  Into the early hours

  Poems.
  ISBN 1-55192-498-6

  I. Title.
PS8565.U5766157 2001   C811'.6   C2001-910853-2
PR9199.4.H85157 2001

Polestar, an Imprint of Raincoast Books
9050 Shaughnessy Street
Vancouver, British Columbia
Canada V6P 6E5
www.raincoast.com

At Raincoast Books we are committed to protecting the environment and to the responsible use of
natural resources. We are acting on this commitment by working with suppliers and printers to
phase out our use of paper produced from ancient forests — this book is one step towards that goal.
It is printed on 100% ancient-forest-free paper (100% post-consumer recycled), processed chlorine-
and acid-free, and supplied by New Leaf Paper; it is printed with vegetable-based inks by Friesens.
For further information, visit our website at www.raincoast.com. We are working with Markets Initiative
(www.oldgrowthfree.com) on this project.

1 2 3 4 5 6 7 8 9 10

Printed and bound in Canada

for Glenn

"Whatever we are now, we were then.
Some days those maps collide ..."

— Michael Ondaatje

"Down through the bedded mouth of the loft trapdoor,
The loosening fodder-chute, the aftermath ..."

—Seamus Heaney

CONTENTS

2   All The Old Thinking

3   What We Saw Having Come Through the Other Side

1

That Green Country

"How do I know my country? Let me tell you,
it has been hard to do."

—EAVAN BOLAND

In Leaving Ireland, What Is Lost

The Irish landscape has marked our bodies:
History written on our flesh as if we were vellum.
It's like the Bufo toad, sloughing off, swallowing his skin;
Layers thin as rice paper adhere to the lining of his mouth.
And we swallow our own skin, our tongues
Moving thick in our mouths against stone walls, valleys, rain.
We are drinking that green country everyday.
A toad tasting what it means to be a toad.
Swamp and lily, his own poison.

What We Have

There is no pure history, only a mess of it, a muddling,
and like soup — Agnes taking this and that from the garden,
adding broad beans and chicken stock, stirring —
everything together arrives. The family at the dinner table
says nothing. But if who we are was known, traceable,
a straight stalk of wheat from root to chaff,
we could say this is the gleaning of our history,
here is the one church, our sins and glories ascribed
to that country, there. We could give them conversation,
the timbre of a voice.

Her kneading leaves flour dust on the breadboard,
round finger-marks the only certainty in a place so new.
In the morning there are fresh loaves and treacle on the table.
Outside Agnes is sowing, and the goose makes for her loose hem,
just missing. The children watch from the kitchen, giggling;
one of the girls presses her nose against glass.
Our history is in between their thoughts and gestures,
still as yet to be made. It's like the moment bread rises in the oven
before settling back in on itself. It's what we break open.

Sunday, the family sets out with baskets to lunch
along the strand. Seven of them in a wood boat, cresting.
Over grey-capped waves, silt stirred up from the bottom, they row.
If the water was clear, we could dip our hands into the whirl
and taste it. Dry wet palms on the picnic blanket, recount unerring
what we know. Instead, they move with the boat as it rolls,
and let list for a moment between shores. They are neither
here nor there, and in no hurry. The sough of the strait
a low whistle around them. When the boat sways again
they will pick up the oars, the slice and pull of moving forward.

Christening

A well out past the rickety grey rot-wood barn,
yoke to help balance two tin buckets of water,
marks red as the lash left across your shoulders
and felt well into supper that evening,
when your father swung the axe at the main post
and you, your mouth full of string beans
heard the slow death-moan of stubborn rafters;
and although he built a paddock,
a small flap-door hen house, there was always
short grass and mud, border of thistle bush.

One January he burned the hens alive, and her
wedding dress, white apron, tea towels with them.
His thin hair frozen to his head with sweat
and winter, as it was on the night you were born
when he ran into the flat wheat field and stayed there,
slamming his fist into the snow.
Like the dry cracking of feather and bone, it is
immolation and birth you most remember:
coming out into the sharp farmhouse air
her blood cold on you, even then.

Clearing Fields

What explosions, going back in time,
can be traced to this:
hedgerow and rubble field
his own astronomical beginning.

First, the stars and her cradling him under them.
Cup and horse, swan, plough,
he followed them as if they were apron strings
would run half a mile towards town
climb the hill before the Burren;

anything better than the house,
all matter converging there,
even light unable to escape up the chimney
find its way out under curtains.
A place even the mice did not enter.

Better the land that stretches north to the peninsula,
for his picking, miles of stone
each one becoming a star in constellations laid out
around the cow, three sheep, James McFarrell

who sleeps out there in his greatcoat
nights he is too drunk to make his way farther home.

Here, the boy buries his hands in hogweed and pulls,
knowing they will outgrow the work left him,
would rather be hunting rabbits or vole,
hauling wood crates full of whiskey
up the walk to McGann's.

He will stand in that field most of his life, stargazing.
Above him whole constellations that can be
obliterated by a thumbnail.
Planets long dead still pressed into orbit.
Each light overhead the idea of somewhere else.
Each stone a kind of ladder.

Emigration During the Famine

They imagined the land beneath them given over to gorse and sloe,
pastures brusquely taken in increments he could measure,
like the last of the water evaporating in a bowl on the sill —
the pony's trough invisible under shrubs of black branches;
although if he traced back the days he could say there was a time
it was clear and full. The field grown into a wild garden
without pathways, well-springs festering under the soil.

She stood on the porch, thumbs hooked over her apron,
saying: once the clearing came to here — flat fields in summer,
grass the colour of mustard set up against the hills.
Saw their house grown over until only an open door remained,
until standing on the last tether of land they gave in.
So they said the country gone wild had overcome them

even though they trekked through open spaces, abandoned
gable houses, those obdurate headstones cropping up in bare fields.
They dragged their belongings behind them, thrashed at
undergrowth that did not exist, thicket paths, the brown calyxes
of flowers thick as a blanket. Until they ran down to the dockyard,
the ship, its wood planks bent to a point, hull settled in water.

Up the gangway, his hand held out behind him,
her bruised and scraped legs twisting in the sway of her skirt.
Stumbling forward she fell hard against the soil, saw
the brown trousered backs of his legs a few feet beyond.
They were moored for hours but already felt the get-away
a lumbering shift beneath them, as if set down under the covers,
newborn. The bassinet, with a touch of the hand, sent rocking.

We Sailed From The Harbour of Leith on the 4th June

Awakened with a cry of John O'Groats, we rallied ourselves,
came out from under blankets, port side and watching,
sailed right past it across Pentland Firth, Agnes almost ready,
and the captain offering his cabin, when the time drew near.
That night we lost sight of Scotland.
And three days later, mid-squall, she delivered of a daughter,
while I pulled buckets of water from the sea,
used her night dress to clean the baby, then set them in their berth,
the whole of the ship rocking.
For weeks we saw nothing but water.
More than once I wondered if we might not be lost altogether.
There was little for comfort and less room with the child,
though Agnes was mending well.
We saw a great shoal of porpoises, the sea wind blew west.
Then the call of the new country, and the lot of us, crowding the rails,
saw how wholly covered by wood it was, spanning the horizon
in either direction, as if a great length of outstretched arms.
So, blessed be God for his mercies and this, my foot set down,
an impression, indelible as we set out on land.

Raising Up

Five of them
taking down the tree.

Himself, his brothers.
An afternoon in August.
They chipped at it, then
split the wood.

There was a slow exhalation
like the kind he'd made
over the porcelain basin
that morning
before the sun was up —
all the night's dreams
rushing out in a sigh,
the splash of cold water
falling back into the cup
of his hands.

His fist was still
around the saw.

Space divided by timber
equals space.
A sprawling emptiness.
The four of them
crouched around the plot
for the shanty, its land
a split-open wound.

His thoughts
were of morning,
the clearing to come.
Now only a stump
remained.

And the wood, it made
a solid coffin.

Naming the Ground

My father has named the ground we walk on:
Angel Shale, Sandstone, Limestone, Schist.
We watch it rise around us, inch by inch it twists,
turning into Olympian Mountains — the Rockies, the Himalayas,
pushing up out of still oceans like craggy sea monsters
poking at the round of the moon.

These are the ghosts of pre-history, their white bones
bared in the wall of every great canyon, coconico —
rounded streaks like ribs. Geologists riding them,
climbing up through layers of time,
remember the Cambrian sea as if they'd been there,
seen those oceans teeming with life.

My father collects in jars the ground we walk on,
filling up his study until our house smells as dark
as the rock-cut tomb of an Assyrian king.
Skeletons line our bookcase: a hare, a sparrow,
the left hand of a man who walked the earth
some ten-thousand years before us.

This summer we stood in the mouth of the Grand Canyon
and pointing to the north ridge my father said:
There are the bones of our ancestors —
trilobites, molluscs and brachiopods.
This stone, kaibab, was made from the dust of their shells,
two hundred and fifty million years ago

or yesterday.
The two of us standing there, small for the first time,
the dry land cracking like skin beneath us.
My father with his hands, words that made
significance of these things. Our eyes to the sky,
cloudless, immense and smooth, like the underside
of a great fish.

Coming Of Age

It's here under the stern of the boat, that thing you reach for,
a glimmer, and even bent at the waist, the curve of wood
cutting into your gut, you cannot reach low enough,
can only dip your fingers in and out of the drift,
can only be pulled back into your seat by your mother's hand,
while she berates herself for turning away to the lunch boxes,
for trusting your father, whose eyes are cast out to the lure
of a fishing line.

"You might've gone right over," your father says,
already imagining the accident, hauling you up
by the belt loops; already seeing his dark arms go under,
fingers stretching to grab hold. "Might have been it," he repeats,
his back to you, knowing by the dip of the boat
that you've returned to your seat, crossed your arms,
are kicking dirty water around on the metal floor.

"The last breath," he concludes, half smiling. Your mother
handing him his sandwich without meeting his eyes.
And after he sets the fishing rod between his knees, the line
still slack, he turns, winks once as if daring you to do it again
as if it's a game you can play, like jumping from the tree house
to the ground.

You take your sandwich, toss the crust in bits
over the side of the boat, hoping the swish-tailed trout
will swim to the surface, jump, a great gleam of muscle
flailing in your arms. You want to be ready when the time comes.
But only the green seaweed lolls up, like so many hands,
fingers unfurling. You lean forward again, as if to grab hold.
The faraway centres of their palms open then shut.

Climbing Lessons

Hand over hand I climbed the ladder of my grandfather's body,
the leg braces under his brown trousers like steps
to a tree house, the only way up — the arch of my bare foot
finding the metal circle around his ankle, my toes curling over it,
that thin band as familiar as a favourite pair of shoes.

Then my left knee making for his lap, for the top of his leg brace,
leverage to haul myself up, like our dog's collar
one summer when she pulled me, holding on, up a hill.
There was never any turning back, no hoisting by the arms.
In my grandfather's house you did things of your own volition.

His hand a compass, how he would tap his chest, say 'come here'
as I crawled over mountains to see him, to stretch out
in the hammock of his arms, bury my head between shirt and cardigan.
The thrum of his heart in my ear, intake of breath like wind
at the tent flaps. And I waited there, eyes closed,

made mental lists of the provisions I would need to get home.
The cuff of his sweater a handhold, the pleats of his pants a kind of rope.
It was up there I said my prayers before sleeping, never sure
of where we were as he walked around the house. That darkness
like a country I wanted to enter.

Sometimes the rain came like hands tapping on the roof, then
the trickling stream of runoff from the gutters, all the sounds of the house
wrapped around us like a blanket. While outside the porch light
shone like a sun busy in other hemispheres. My grandfather moving
into the place beyond it, long after I'd climbed down.

Mendel's Garden

The garden is a language, an old tongue he is trying to learn —
stigma, stamen, sepal, the pure red of the petals in front of him,
Mendel in the far beds behind the monastery, saying the words
over and over again, a latinate hymn, an invocation,
campanula, matthiola, fuchsia; the bright eyes of God
     watching him.

A carpet of flowers this summer, the garden ready to burst,
the bees burrowing themselves in the throats of flowers,
the cloister wall hidden behind the climbing rose bush.

     He is avoiding the greenhouse.

The garden peas give him nothing these days but grief.
And he is always on his knees in there, has spent half his time
at the monastery leaning over, tying pea stalks to lattice,
measuring their growth, reseeding them, transplanting,
whole generations the work of his hands.

Perhaps this is penance, a desire for order in a chaotic world,
or his own petition, day after day watering the plants
as if he could coax them out of their dark secret.

His hands on them, his breath on them;
but in the evening he goes to bed with their scent on him,
sweet must, wet earth, remnants of pollen. *Pisum sativum*,
pedicel, placenta: in his dreams the garden peas
climb up towards the glass ceiling of the green house.

There is no one else to do this work, no one with the patience,
they are only peas to the others. But Gregor sees something else,
how like us they are, savouring the comfort of the womb
but born anyway, into their own ingenuity, variation,
the propagation that is almost speech.

Shoulders

My father must have carried me on his shoulders,
although I don't remember. There are so many photos
of my sister in his arms or slung over his shoulder
and one in his red convertible when she was two or three
and he'd set her in the passenger seat. Autumn in Sudbury,
a few yellow leaves scattered over the upholstery.

I have my own memory of leaves that must have come
from a good height, how else could I have reached them?
Tugging and twisting at the stems, pulling by the fistful
those mottled flags, ruby-brown spans twice the width
of my hand. Up there I learned the names of trees, touched
the cocoons of caterpillars, those white gauzy strands,
like luminescent tightropes strung between fingers.

This is how I imagine children are shown the world,
their ankles held tight in their father's hands
as they lean and lean forward, reach out between branches,
the canopy of leaves swirling above and the small
dark eyes of birds, watching. The whole world is in that space,
in the way I imagine my father carrying me on his shoulders,
stepping left then right, as if dancing.

How easy it is to look up in memory, at hands and sky
instead of feet. I remember the brown elbows of branches
mid-waltz above me, the spin and whirl as I turned,
sunlight in oblong patterns. A snapshot. I remember
that childhood as if from a great height, the smell of moss
and dust, a thatched nest in the crooked neck of the tree.
The ground coming up to greet me years before I was ready.

Vision of My Mother as Saint Catherine

She is ten or eleven, standing in the playground
in a blue fluted summer dress, hands in pockets
watching the other girls as they grab the rusted railing,
dig their sneakers into the sand,
push the merry-go-round until it's really spinning.

She has ridden it too, in the park after hours,
coming across the street with her sister
who pushes faithfully while she holds the bars,
leans out as far as she can, the whole of the park
turning into a blur of field and trees.

It takes concentration but sometimes she can see
the street lights leaning in the distance
the playground swings anchored in their stillness,
the sand box as open as a grave
and her own tenebrous fate,

a boy who will change her, who will take her
even though this is all she might ever want —
this reeling, the feeling she gets stepping down
as if this world is no place for her, as if it cannot hold her,
as if walking she barely touches the ground.

The Burning Ground

His old coal-shed filled with garden tools,
rake prongs bent in all directions, as if used to pull stone,
the hoe still caked with dry earth;
and my grandfather dying in the house behind me.
I want to bring the garden back for his last summer,
pull up the bindweed, those pale flowers
trellising over the shed like poor man's ivy.
Instead I stand in the mess of shears and trowels
holding the shovel's rough wood handle,
unable to root or dig.

Above ground there are only remnants,
clusters of skullcap and sorrel pushed up
against the house, the daffodil bulbs he didn't bury
recumbent on the flower beds, dandelions in full bloom
congregating around the lawn mower.
If he looks out the window this is what he will have
to remember — the grass grown over, the shed leaning left,
garden tools hung up on rusty nails.

So I spread new seeds, finger-poking holes
all over the yard, hoping for wildflowers, those pods
that split open, come head-first into the world.
But in his bed he is remembering the coal,
lop-sided stacks shovelled into a tin bucket before the war,
winters warmed by the black lung of the furnace,
char dust catching in the lines of his palm.
A black rock the size of a heart in his hand,
how he'd curl his fingers over it,
put it in the burner, let go.

In the Field

Standing by the slats in the wood gate,
sagebrush reaches up past my knees, almost burying me,
and burying the hooves of the blind Appaloosa
father tethered in the field.

For years she has stood, bound by the neck
with taut bailing twine he braided like my sister's hair.
Once I thought the rope a wreath of wheat,
a golden halo cut from the field

but it tangles in her mane, tight across shoulders,
curls in on itself in the weather, a pale rattlesnake
I can't wish away. Once we fed her apples and sugar,
those days when she'd butt her nose into the air,

pull hard on her leanings and break them,
making a good run for the back field.
Now there's a patch of worn grass, and like Saturn
she seems dependent on her tether to keep her in orbit.

The noose around the Appaloosa's neck grown into her.
Its threads like skin peeling slowly back, like the splitting
of a cocoon, like the forked vein in my father's arm
when he takes an axe to wood.

I would give up my childhood to have it gone.
That rope a round open mouth, twined into knotted teeth,
her body still behind it, long head hanging
out of that darkness.

Fixed

It's the way a man can stand
on the slope of a roof in the rain

a blowtorch in his left hand, its curled flame
so small against the dark stacks of shingles,

it seems like nothing more than the glint
of a lantern wavering in the wind

and below him the yellowed grass, tufted curl
of moss and lichen, a brown mud welt

at the base of an alder tree where you
stand for a moment, watching him work

in the darkness. It's the way you too reach
down, as if tarring something into place.

One hand against the ordinary
and pressed into the dirt, the warm muck —

this is how things become fixed,

the dark span of your hand, the flicker
of light that comes and goes.

Recollection

The slim-wristed dead are with you again,
in their ruffled blouses and long white skirts —
two young girls, feet slung out of the hammock
on Chatham street, sleeping and as still as fish
too long out of water, mouths open
under a bright canopy of sun. It's late summer
and every afternoon has been like this one

but for your hand on the banister of the back porch,
as incongruous as an airplane in an apple grove.
That you can touch her shoulder and wake her,
along with her sister and the small brown terrier
curled up in the shade. That the oak tree's leaves
feather your neck as you stand beside them.

She wakes up slowly and enters the house
as if it still existed, and the two of them
climb kitchen chairs and pick through the pantry
for snacks. Spread jam on bread then dip their fingers
in the jar. How young they are now,
and how forgotten. Her memories at work in you,
smell of the countryside when you wake.

Upon All The Living and the Dead

— on Joyce

Not the small brown seed that you are,
an epiphany in the grave — mud-mouthed
and hungry for air and incident.
But rather this: snow-covered turf and bog,
preservation less elastic than words,
every aspect of you debated, as if a haggard,
its property line along the Shannon,
two back fields where farmers stand indignant,
hoe and slean in hand —
that they might strike low and break you open.
Then how steadfast that litany
of root and stalk returns.

After the Irish Republican Releases

Wasted, although now you see how
monuments might have been made,
built on that out-crop of land,
its sometimes appearing peninsula,
sea-green swells breaking over spare earth.

You will have that colour on you always,
a damp haunting. Like the licks of grass
and ivy tendril that made way up the prison walls.
And though you look in pockets, along the seams
of your coat, you find no trace of it, no dark stain,
only a sense that the ebb tide is in you.

Everywhere this rolling backward,
induction of breath, dissuasion.
Men etch obstinate capital I's in concrete,
mark days, while you argue hands against stone,
dig tunnels that cave in, grow moss-laden
with time.

So too our lives run their course behind us,
slow enough, we could excavate ourselves.

You remember the story of the old bog man,
his body, puckered and bound, churned over
by tillers and broken. They pulled him from the peat
by his neck, and when clear they washed him,
touched the thin trails of veins pressing up against skin,
like byroads arriving nowhere and everywhere at once.

Now you name those fixed desires: to rise above,
appear not as a ghost but as a man,
his own drowning behind him.

Take in everything you see — the hedgerows,
motorway to Belfast, its thoroughfares,
the fallow ground beyond.
There is a rising in you yet. A turning over.
You have come off the teetering bluff,
its spindrift erosion, out from the headland,
back into the world.

After Having Loved that Country

After having loved that country like blood burst in the brain,
the leaving of it made light-headed in the up and up,
these hands pressed hard on the window of good-bye.

But and small, we are gestures and only in this anything,
the tiniest untunneling of words from the mouth,
the mechanism of howl, and how, after having loved

the air indifferent tumbles back in our absence
as if we, like arms open and heart, its red and mad going,
had never loved that land, whole body desiring to stay.

The Great Irish Poets Mark My Passing

Heaney, Healy, Boland, Durcan and Mahon
on the Sligo-Dublin road near Mullingar.
They've given up the car and are walking.

There's been a cask of stout between them
and now they argue the politics of words.
How to best describe a tern, an ocean wake,
a young girl.

"I knew a girl," Durcan says, "in Canada.
I've just had news of her death."
"What kind of girl?" asks Healy,
all of them wanting a good invocation —
it's not every day you write an epitaph.

"A solid girl," says Durcan, "a poet
in my class. Outspoken in some ways but —"
he pauses, "sturdy in the hips."

No one says anything for some time.
Stones are kicked towards Lough Ennell.
Boland considers the return to earth.
"We'll mourn," she says, "with a pissing contest."

Heaney'd had the most to drink.

"I knew a girl," Durcan says, "in Canada,"
relieving himself on some bungalow lawn.
All of them pissing with vigor
as if they could win me back from the dead
before carrying on.

Going Against Yeats

> *'A picture does not need translation. It does not need documentary evidence,*
> *dates, photographs of the artist or what he says about his pictures.*
> *It does not matter who or what I am.'*
>
> —JACK YEATS

It's always the horse with you, this time riderless —
quick white brushstrokes against a stretch of heather,
gorse like sun laid out on the hills.

A ghost of a horse heading towards you,
wisp of flank, splatter of mane,
and an eye so wildly drawn it might be

alder burl or amber, might be basalt or blood,
the cup of your hands in the evening basin,
the dark house you walked away from.

This is what you give us — a pale horse
that won't be broken, a wide open country road,
the land furrowed in both directions

and nothing but sky above us,

and only this horse before us,

and the far off machinery that makes her run.

2

All the Old Thinking

"All the new thinking is about loss.
In this it resembles all the old thinking."

—Robert Hass

Thoughts of Able-Bodied Seaman Garrow
after the Dispatch

(One hundred and five men died after abandoning ship
in Arctic waters on the failed Franklin expedition, 1848)

Walk.
Everywhere white, and starting out
you are newborn as if this is the first
moment and you have come great lengths
to face it. Your own insignificance
astounds you and even staring at your hands,
the broadcloth and twine around them,
you cannot imagine what use
they might have been made for.
If only you are steadfast, a sure-footed way
might be found. At least, moving forward,
you can say: I am here and living,
each step an arrival, untread.
And soon enough, God allowing, you'll find
a seat at the mouth of Back's Fish River,
its clear water the edge of ice.
You might live to see this ending,

to chart further course, all the way
through to the Pacific.

Men stumble along behind you
although there is no opening
for voices here. Shout, and the sound
is lost, carried underground, held in
that thin pearl space between water
and a slate that spreads North,
pressing into grey corners of sky.
Know that you have arrived at all points,
where the man you have come to be is
bested, the wind against your chest
like hands laid against you.
Consider now the things you've carried
and what you chose to leave behind,
but mourn nothing in the face of this
greatness, the white field spread before you
as if you could leap into time
and watch yourself. A man set down
on the edge of the world,
the possible before him.

Frank Slide, Alberta

(*The town of Frank was buried in a rock avalanche
at Turtle Mountain in Alberta, 1903*)

You will hover above that town
all your afterlife, almost touching,
and remember, it was there we planted
clusters of snap-dragons and tulips,
and above us, burrowed under
the eavestrough spout,
a hornets' nest buzzed furiously
through summer.
And you, earth-stained
in the garden, hoe in hand, laughing
said you didn't have the heart
to knock it down.
Savoured the clipped sound
of their stingers against the kitchen glass,
like the small stones I'd thrown
up to your bedroom window
from your parents' front yard.

That summer the morning glory
overtook everything
and you spent hours untangling
the open blossoms, one from the other.

We were nothing next to that power,
swell of earth upturned —
and I choose to imagine you were
wrapped warm in the light
blue sheets you'd taken off the line,
smell of field grass still in them.
It was as if the ground gave
a great yawn at the end of an evening
before slumber.
And then a blanket, and under
the stony plain not a murmur or sigh.
Even the flowers bowing down
to a new loneliness.

The Panchen Lama

Somewhere in a room without windows
the Panchen Lama sits
imagining the time of day, remembering
the fall of light across his mother's face
the afternoon the soldiers took them,

how she had to close her eyes against it,
sunlight coming in through the canvas flap
at the back of the truck, the dust
from the road catching in their throats.

This is grief and something else—
a longing that exists outside the body
it is the way birds want to be the wind
they pass through, the way we hold
what we cannot contain.

The room is cold and the Panchen Lama shivers.
He is just a boy from a rural village,
a child without means to count the years.
Later he might remember

the number of times birds settled on the roof,
how the cooing pigeons calmed him, he might
go back to the one day they led him out
into the back garden, how there were colours
blooming there he thought he'd never seen.

A way of accounting, each petal
reinvented in his mind, the whole
of a single flower months in the making,
a face from the village a matter of years.

He knows they will never free him
and they cannot kill him. He is given just enough —
the sounds of birds, wind storms, a door that opens
when the woman comes to feed him,
a glimpse through the window in the room beyond.

Outside he knows there are knots of long grass,
a dirt path that heads towards the city
and somewhere foothills
that ache upwards, out of themselves,
turning, in the distance, to mountains.

Carl Jung At Eighty-Three

Resting in bed at Bollingen,
Carl Jung remembers the body:
a boy laid out in the dark womb of the wash house,
a candle lantern strung up above his head.

He remembers standing outside
on an upturned bucket, peering through the window,
studying the boy's gaping mouth,
the blond head wrenched sideways,
a gash that almost tore the chin right off.

It had to have happened the moment after —
the boy descending Rhine Falls
as if it was a banister he could slide down,
the cluster of rocks at the bottom
like the slap of his father's hand.

Blood and water trickled out the drain
behind the wash house and kneeling down
Carl cupped it in his hands, tasted it —
lye tinged with mud and what he thinks of now
as marrow.

Gripping the wood frame window,
clambering up for a better view,
he saw a straw basket full of white linen,
two of his father's shirts hanging stiffly on the line
and the shawl in which his mother
sometimes wrapped him, pegged up by the door.

There was blood in all of this and Carl knew
even then, this boy from the village
was in him too, he knew it the way he knew
the boy's mother would come running
and with gentle hands try to raise her son.

This is his first memory as a boy:
his father walking towards him
across the lawn in Laufen
a dark-haired woman trailing behind,
the window cracked at its brace
and the boy's mouth;
and somewhere near the gardens,
his father calling his name.

Happenstance

Paula Modersohn-Becker to Rainer Maria Rilke

I write, *It was not everything I thought it would be*—
as if explaining Paris, the dark maroon
of the flat, curtains flailing in the fist of wind,
barrelling through the guttered window.

And, *What we make we must throw away*
because our secrets come loudly out
even as our eyes are closed against them.

I remember you at the old wood table
in the kitchen. Pouring the last of the wine
as if we were not struggling, as if paints could be
procured as readily as words. What could I say then
that did not reveal me? We were open wounds,
obeying the formalities of a meal.

I arrived in Worpswede for the weekend with Otto
and he asked after your well-being.
I spoke of your adeptness with oyster shells

and language, of the small curling words
you wrote in my journal after dinner.
Buttery finger-marks left on the page.

I think of that last flickering of light,
the hiss as you pinched the wick of the candle
after writing. Smoke curling around,
finding its way to the nearest draft.
The dishes left stranded on the table.
All that rain coming in.

I do not want to know how you see me,
and as a gesture will never paint you again
will pretend art is an exercise of the wrist
and not the chipped wineglass you sent
tumbling over, broken in two on the floor.

Both halves just set there, one lying next
to the other. A rut of wine left in the hollow.
The knock of loose shutters against the August gloom,
their clap, the sound of a heart beating.
You and I, and our useless hands.

Night Train to London

The train charges on past Durham, and the conductor
marks our tickets, moves past us into the next car.

You haven't said a word since you sat down beside me
in Edinburgh. A man lost in the rhythm of the train.

Now, examining your hands, you slowly turn them over,
touch one, then the other, fingers pressing gently into palms.

You say they were buried in the North Sea eight hours ago,
off the coast of Aberdeen — third oil rig to go up this year.

First time you were dropped from a helicopter,
to a boat a mile from the explosion.

From far away, you say, the water seemed littered
with the light of campfires.

Between them you reached over the side of a Zodiac,
searching for bodies, finding five.

Only twenty-nine years old and already you feel your skin tighten,
close in on your body. Hands still sore and burning from the cold.

The train is surging on to London. But I keep going back
to your arms lost in the blackness of the sea.

I want to rescue you, a stranger, as if I can pull you on board,
grab the back of your jacket, haul you in.

But we are both in that body of water now.

And beyond the window, the blur of city lights
offers no comfort. We are moving toward them anyway—

lighthouses in the distance, tiny pyres we look to,
pass by, but cannot reach.

Claude Monet Stopping at Gare du Nord

There is not, head willing, enough time for this,
a study like any other. The moment dissipates and is gone.
The arrival of comprehension — light, and no more
than the most pedestrian miracle,
two francs in the pocket after years of starvation,
the first stroke of blue on canvas.

We must hold tight-fisted our own slippery revenants:
a leaf curling perfectly, an August afternoon.
What reveals us, in an instant, alone and slight —
time a station, unexpected and soon.
So my hands around these coins,
how they glimmer against the skin.

William Morris in the Glassworks with Jane

You and I amongst this madrigal of hands,
furnace like a tongue of fire, thick-throated,
and all around us light blown by men and spun.
The room held just so, sweet ruby quarrels,
chalk dust along the baseboards.
And oh, but for the line of your neck in this,
swan, I half expect your palm to feather my hand
when you reach for it.

The glaziers here hover over work, silent
as death we pass crucifixion and resurrection,
the apology of angels for wings,
when we, our fingers medieval and bone,
can cut life from air, even making it,
as you have made me, solid.
Air and this — the rustle of your skirts lifted
over the door sill, choirs bursting under my skin.

3

What We Saw,
Having Come Through the Other Side

"*The longer you look at a thing,*
the more it transforms."

—Anne Michaels

He Comes Home from the War

In the valley the wind has its own measure,
courses down to burrow the old river bottom,
splays the spear grass, the brome,
wends them into cowlicks, spun stalks,
weather vanes.
                    And the hill above
is the slumbering body of a man
who went out through stable doors
carrying the lantern of the moon,
who cut across the prairie leaving rifts
in his wake.

He has come home from the war,
a battered suitcase held together with rope,
a lost letter, he has come home
and his wounds have made him
more than he was, have made him
                    a barrow,
the wind over the fields,
the railway cutting through, steel tracks,
the long sight of a gun, wheat pressed out
in all directions.

Lying down in the grass he counts the passing
sparrows, waits for them to circle back, land.
He watches the glinting sun on wings,
works his hands into the cracked earth,
cups roots in his palm,
                              sage and thistle
sentinel around him,
the valley a cut-away, birch-treed trench
at his feet.

When he finally goes to ground
the birds will stutter and land, fold their wings
over him, they will know him,
as if he'd always been there,
                              a gently sloping hill,
fossil, fox hole, blood stone,
under the burl of milk vetch,
under rock cress and yarrow.

A Forecast, the Weather

Old stone white-washed cottage, the floor sloped and the cat
with his three legs, and you remembering it was always so,
believe in phantom limbs for balance.

This spring the roof was reft by the wind
and the weather trowelled in evenly over the arborite table,
wool blankets, the nattered couch.

These four rooms that were once a house and then a barn.
You and old Conneely taking the mule out with a rope
around her neck despite the awful craning, guttural moans.

On leaving she kicked in a square of wall across from the doorway.
Tufts of her hair still worked into cracks of stone.
All this rain coming in.

Rusted buckets, then a black tarp that keeps us up
with its flap, its flitter at night. Ours an alate cottage,
an awkward crow caught in coastal gusts.

In two years you'll be dead and already we feel it
like something grown between us, cold to the touch —
a blanket with holes, a dark gleam that billows for sky.

The old chimney tossing loose stones over the tarp
as if skimming them across water. Oh how we feel the pull
of those pebble-strewn banks on us,

note the four walls, panes of glass giving in,
those curled hands of foam combing the Bay
when we walk out to it.

The haggard ocean laid out before us
and the moon gone down to the slit of an eye.
The clouds close to clearing, even so.

At This End of the Country

My home is made
at this end of the country

an Island in a fistful
of Islands

the maple and arbutus
laying down

and the currents
quick to change.

Under Christchurch Bells

Tonight it's cold, and the wind whips around me,
makes whooshing sounds down the front of a four-storey building
where a woman stands in her window
hanging clothes over the radiator — two shirts, a yellow blouse —
        the Denman bus suddenly passing between us,
        its engine rumbling into traffic, a row of faces
        staring out at the street.
It's eight p.m. and over the city the bells of Christchurch
Cathedral start ringing.

        But something is wrong.
The clang and brawn of the bells fall out of tune and order,
without remorse, like an argument between the bell ringer and God,

the clamour peeling out from the tower, and all of us
on the street and in our houses look over: see a dark steeple,
the quick glint of its bells.

Tolling, they sound out over False Creek, climb the hill
towards Kitsilano, the noise like a bull run through town,
stopping only at dead-ends and doorways,

the ground reverberating, and panes of glass in the barber shop,
the mini-mart windows warble with each hard note.

There are countries where towns are still built around their churches.
Houses and shops fanning out like a crinoline skirt from the body,
towns where bells ring out over everyone and everything
in even benediction —

The woman in her window looks towards the cathedral
and the buses on Pender idle alongside the road;
the chestnut trees have filled with birds suddenly afraid to fly.

In the bell tower hands pull hard on ropes
that are capable of music,
                    but perhaps this too is a song,
the hands belonging to a man who is finding his place
in the middle of this city,
who finds a chorus of open mouths with him,
ringing out against the hour.

End of the Season

The coyotes have come down into the city
and travel on coarse pads into the silence
between buildings, into the shaft of darkness
between our lean-to shed and the one plank
of wood nailed into a rotted stump,
that passes for a fence. This the season
for generosity, the time of the year when
the compost is good foraging,
when the leaf blowers are packed away
and shovels are brought up from basements
to wait like Southern travellers for snow.
The weather its own sort of miracle,
a string of nights so clear and cold, the Bay
could have been mistaken for sky, and was,
how standing on the beach at Stanley Park
I almost stepped into it, a liquid field of quartz stars.

This year there is talk of the millennium,
as if time itself will hinge in the last hours
of December, then swing open like an old door
into a new room. Our linearity a mixed blessing
and nights like these, ones you can pass through
with certainty, the same.
Outside, the coyotes nose through husk and rind
while the house falls dark with evening,
above us the moon like light through a keyhole —
the coyotes looking up to it from their forage
and to the black slate that could be sky,
ocean or doorway, or a field so speckled with frost
it glints as the coyotes lift their heads,
pause between steps.

My Neighbour's Yard

Tulips like a lawn that cropped up
red and yellow of its own volition,
or a hundred brightly beaked birds

their green wings floundering,
arced like drooped shoulders,
like a woman caught undressing.

My neighbour a Dutch expatriate
or, I imagine, a clock maker,
woodcarver, someone consumed

with how things fall away.
His shutters always open to it,
as if surveying the lilt of land

the language flowers speak in.
How they grow tired of all that
standing up, being counted.

The petals bursting open, shout,
argue amongst themselves,
arc their heads until you can see

down their throats. Even the bees
feed off their anger, the whirr
of dropped expletives.

We are not oblivious, catch,
out of the corner of our eyes, this yard
with its wide open mouth,

with its battalion of measured living.
Theirs is a colloquial equilibrium,
and ours is like that too, we are

the man standing in his open doorway,
the old clock, the slow metronome of
days. And passing we are

one foot off the curb, lost in the clamour
of voices. The tulips bending over,
making way to the ground.

Thoughts on Marriage

A jar of wet earth,
a bulb burst open
its roots banded around
the inside of the glass.

Thin streams of ribbons,
tendriled hands.

The window box brimming
in its square of sunlight,
the flowers' dark throats
like bell glasses full of wine.

Riding Through Fernwood at Night

The whirr of bike tires,
white mutt loping along behind us —

and other than our sometimes conversation,
the streets carry no sound,

only the crunch of maple and oak leaves
threshed under tires

the dim hum of electrical lines
trussing the city.

Ours is a neighbourhood of hills,
every street corner giving way

to steep inclines, downward slopes,
houses that lean into the furl

of their shrubbery.

This is our valley, very unlike the one
in which we were married:

        ragweed and heather flung out for miles,
        blur of sheep shouldering the hill,
        the fold and tow of field grass,
        as we rode the bus to the village.

The bride's account:

        Near comedy, our wedding, how I
        almost missed it — took the wrong train
        from Androssen, didn't make the last ferry;
        how I tripped up the aisle anyway,
        handed off in due time by Alistair MacAlistair
        your Scottish uncle, a man whose hands
        could cover the Mull of Kintyre.

The groom's account:

        All things being equal, we stood
        the tempest, we stemmed the tides;
        though I had my doubts,
        the ship came in and we were landed.

Now we live on a plateau and the city
swells out around us, oblivious to

late night bicycle rides, the acorns strewn
across Denman and the dog

who races across someone's lawn,
clearing a low wall before turning for home.

The porch light on as we walk our bikes
up the path, hear the clap of the gate

behind us. The bride's account.
The groom's account.

Either way, a valley. And the slope,
the climb, of what comes after.

Driving the River

All that trip we were pushed up against the river,
driving beside the mountain, along those logging roads
where we veered around bends like a rudderless boat,
stones lapping up into the wheel-wells, a steel ricochet;

the Fraser, its drunken swagger, an open mouth
taking everything in, the stand of trees on either side
ripped from the banks by their roots. Two dozen birches
butting up and down in the current like a raft
pulled apart at the seams.

     We drove up past the snowline and then
     under it more times than I can remember
     and with every turn, the flat of Seton Lake
     swung in and out of view below us,
     a small handbag on the hip of the Fraser

     where we waded into the reeds
     threw sticks the dog wouldn't retrieve,
     each of them lumbering a while
     before catching the current,
     tumbling downstream.

If we hadn't taken the wrong road we might have
missed the crib of Terzaghi Dam, two towns slung
like tassels below it; might have missed the old tavern
and the confetti of houses thrown up the mountain,
or the pipeline we walked along, its throat
braced by girders and the moon.

       That night we found a brown snake
       making its long 's' across our campsite.
       You picked it up with a branch,
       tossed it into the woods

       and we marvelled
       at its yellow belly, how it stretched
       those last few seconds, almost seemed
       to hurl itself headlong into the wind,
       the cool green ribs of fern.

On our last day, after two hours of weaving downhill,
we came out bottom to the smell of burning brakes,
and a picnic table along the river where we sat,
listened to the engine tick and cool, eyed the wire nets
knitting loose stones against the crag;

the whole Cariboo poised against falling, against
the water winding its way down, a trickle
as thin as ore veined through the guts
of the mountain behind us. Now and then the sound
of rocks tumbling down, stones careening
as they headed to the river, cartwheeled and dropped.

Stepping Out of the Possible

On the side of the road a man wearing a white shirt,
jeans and trainers loads boxes into the back of his panel van,
disappearing into the black mouth of it like Jonah;
the panel van parked at the corner of Mackenzie and 41st,
in front of a stop sign, so when the dump truck comes
barrelling down the road, the driver doesn't see it,
heads straight through the intersection —

and the village is going about its business, my husband and I
at the bakery doorway, a woman walking her retriever
on the far side of the road.

Predetermined, or luck of the draw, that the woman
in the red Honda stops halfway across Mackenzie,
feels the rumbling or some sixth sense well up in her
like a sorrow she has to pause over,
pushes her brakes down and then suddenly looks up,
the grey wall of the truck looming, large as a movie screen,
replaying every moment in her life that mattered.

The dump-truck driver laid down black treads as he tried to veer,
last minute, around her, his tires squealing and my heart
thrumming up in my ears, the retriever going wild
with the tension. Jonah coming back out of the whale
wondering at all the commotion —

in that one split second we were all dead
behind the wheel of someone else's accident.

No one heard the hit, the well of his tire against her bumper,
no one felt the pull of the car but her,
the way it bowed down, bounced off the asphalt,
no one saw her thrust her arm across the passenger seat
to protect a child who was not there;
this is all reiteration, a retracing of steps, it's the way
we can't see what's going to happen, can only guess at it,
put our foot down on the brake, pull apart those first moments after —

the woman with the dog running up to the car window,
the baker coming outside with flour on his hands,
all of us walking towards the accident
to step out of the possibility of our own fate,
secure ourselves in details that don't belong to us:

an Asian woman, a red car, a street we have never
driven down, a dump truck full of other people's debris,
dust layering the air like storm clouds.

The truck door opens and the car door opens and the man
in the panel van comes forward, stands in the street
knowing he is to blame, thanking God for this near miss,
forgetting that danger lies as much in the imagination.

He looks at our faces, at the woman leaning against
her car door, then back to his van.
He pulls off his cap, smoothes back his hair,
comes forward into a bright afternoon intersection,
measuring the distance from guilt.

The Bed You Made

The bed you made from a chestnut tree.
Four poster, canopy. Bevelled rails bending
in and out like branches.
Over them you draped soft fabric,
cut from a sari the colour of sky.
Because we had bedposts for the first time
you tied my wrists with black tights,
the sash from your terry cloth bathrobe.

You entered me there, in the middle
of the chestnut tree. Pried open, the soft core
exposed. You entered me in that darkness,
the smell of cut wood still in your hair.
My hands tied to the body of timber,
fists balled, their roundness like shelled chestnuts.
You braced yourself against the bedposts
and I could not put my arms around you.

Scorsese's Last Temptation of Christ

It must be transfiguration, that dream
where Willem Dafoe is with me
under a mound of blankets,
curled up on the wrong side of my bed.

My knees nudged into the backs of his,
my breasts nestled between his shoulder blades,
and I'm wearing my best pair of flannel pajamas —
the blue ones, white pinstripes.

And suddenly it occurs to me, my hands
palm down against the flat of his chest —
I'm spooning Christ,
so I inch my fingers along, over his ribcage.

They don't hang you on the cross with ribbons,
he tells me, that being the reason why
his hands and feet get so cold,
why he bundles the blankets around them

why he always sleeps on the same side.
Then he turns, opens his arms for me, Willem Dafoe,
and I go in to the smell of sleep, stale gin
the cigarettes he smoked the night before.

Then I turn my back to him, my bum wiggling
into his groin until we are joined perfectly,
until his hands find mine, and he anoints them
with his lips, one finger at a time.

Sleeping With Gwendolyn

— after Gwendolyn MacEwen

I should have slept with him because you had, and it would be a way
of knowing you. You being the one I imagine
saying, *Here, hold me like this*, or *Touch me this way*. And maybe it was
when the two of you were together in his Montreal flat,
bed-springs eking out something you likened to Mozart's "Turkish Finale,"
the horns caught up in their own delirium, only the cymbals missing,
maybe it was then, your hand running over the hill of his back,
that you thought of camels and opened your eyes to him, knowing yourself
an explorer, a TE Lawrence whose legs wrapped around dromedaries,
whose hands were wet with oil spilled from lamps carried at dusk.
Even the cant of his back a new language, an inescapable sigh
meshed with Bedouin tongue. This he gave you.

I should have slept with him, and not for his poetry, his hotels,
the odd white-frame house he writes of,
but for what it was you might have left behind: a drawer full of shirts,
an off-white half-slip, the possibility of a letter where you wrote
All your hands are verbs before it became a poem.
And if I'd found something of him on the way, it would be incidental,
a geography I learned the better to arrive at my destination —
the deserts you tripped through to the middle of nowhere, the hurried

unrolling and raising of tents like a wild spread of limbs,
and beyond that, the hollow of a collar bone, where his fingers found you.
That he might place his hands there on me, or lightly over my eyelids,
them saying to you as much as anyone: come, choose, be.

We Go Over It Again

We go over it again the way a horse from habit
or desire circles the paddock wearing down its wheel of grass

and as always I say the words — ask if you're sorry, answer
of course you are without pausing between breaths.

Here, the apple sliced open in the hand, here the tug
on the bridle that leads back to the barn. A nostalgia,

digging in and pulling up all the old dirt until the ground
becomes a series of trenches, even the fence posts falling in.

The problem with infidelity is the loss of borders,
set maps, roads once navigated turn into nowhere, towns disappear

even the bed takes on the wrong geography; the road out past
the window revealing unfamiliar figures in the distance,

cut-out against the meadow-light, everyone facing the one direction
as if waiting for a train. The couch grass and clover bend,

people move towards their destinations and we go over it again
though the horse is tired and the barn leans in architectural empathy

or maybe from neglect or longing; but the paddock stands,
we make sure of it, and in the barn the horse waits through darkness

for daylight and the fence again, the half-turn that's never completed,
the familiar landscape reigned in.

Distance

We are standing in an old metal shed
on the hill behind the monastery.
Twenty feet away the friar who built it is buried,
along with the old cat who'd followed him in
from Lumsden one winter, begging for scraps.
There is a telescope here and a cut-a-way
in the dome of the shed, the night sky a swath
above us, the Perseid meteors skimming across it
like the stones we tossed over Old Wives Lake
that summer when I was four and you were ten,
and the spear grass grew up past my shoulders.

A group of us huddles around the telescope,
near-strangers moving closer for warmth.
The wind coming over the field rattles the walls,
the odd tin flex sounding out like made-for-TV thunder
while the astronomer shows us star clusters,
binary twins, a bright nebula uneven and blurry
like an oblong birthmark set against newborn skin.
Then he names galaxies, recites distances,
the number of years it takes a point of light to reach us.

It will take me two hours to get to Saskatoon
if the roads are clear, although I can count the number
of times I've turned around, the miles between us,
the fields fanning out between farms,
the porch lights like familiar constellations.
The stars know nothing of this, how we find these
awkward orbits, how we once stood outside this shed,
two months married, eyeing the perigee of the moon.

The door of the shed has been left open, and outside
brome and meadow turn under September,
grassland bending into itself as far as the eye can see.
I walk towards the car knowing the impassable
still stands between us, and for the first time
I can measure the distance from this patch of prairie
to everywhere else I have ever been.
It is that dark stretch bridging stars, the fields
of wheat heading into the night around me;
those stalks leaning over in the fist of wind.

Walking the Dog

A short-cut through the city, past pot-holes,
the sloped roofs of carports, and now and again,
the outstretched arms of fern
appearing between garbage bins.
I know this hour of the day,
who will be home, what lights will be on,
how the black Jetta will reverse into the garage
at five-forty p.m.
These alleyways, the back doors of people's lives,
unswept and cluttered, the grass growing over
the edge of the patio, the cat passing hours
pressing her cheek against glass.

The dog trots ahead of me, and the noise of traffic
swells around us, rush hour heading down roads
on the far side of these houses.
I hear tin cans clattering into the recycle,
a window sliding into its latch.
The mongrel down the block bays again
and above us power lines hum, split the sky
into horizons, a series of wide screens

the birds wing across before cutting out
in the opposite direction.

Almost winter and these walks are shorter,
the alleys settling into evening like failing lungs,
and even the dog ready to turn home after half an hour,
the raccoons getting ready to make their rounds
as I button my coat up to the chin.
Past us another light flicks on in someone's kitchen,
all of us heading into our own distant lives,
or turning to go home.

This is philosophy, dusk descending like a curtain,
the leaves that mark the lateness of the season
browning in the absence of light,
raked into seams along the edge of the yard.
Here, a row of tomatoes leans into frost
like blood pearls on the vine
and walking the dog I believe the city into being
even though there is only
the fall of light from a bedroom window,
a metal shed, the sound of pots in a kitchen,
to convince me.
The alleyway sloped as we walk along it,
and in parts, lilting.

In Ballyshannon

Half seen in the arc of light tossed up off the Erne
you are with me and I am in Ballyshannon again,
the autumn of two-thousand, a reel of time between us,
whole fields furrowed under, and a length of family
that could span this bridge.

Below us the stones you used to leap across
are pressed down into the silt-bottom and you are
so long dead I can barely imagine what you might have
looked like, can only trace these same streets
you walked along, knowing you follow behind.

By the crossroads there are shops and houses,
new buildings that sprang like teeth from the ground.
And at the end of town, two men who harness a bull
bought at the fair; they are pulling him towards the byre,
rope tight around his neck, his hooves dug into the dirt.
He is all muscle, straining away from the dark lean of the shed.

As we walk past, the farmers are still trying to lead him in,
the anvil of his head butting down,
nostrils working the ground below him.
He is taking in the scent of the men so he'll remember them,
so in the future he'll know they're coming
in the minutes before they arrive.

I have always known you, despite the wood slats
of time between us. You have marked me, and this town
is a kind of light I am driven toward:
the woman whose grandmother knew you
is airing her sheets on the line; and here the cottage you lived in,

and the field you farmed, stretching like old skin,
bared rocks and stone from Bundoran to the Bay.
A kind of tracery, my cutting through town as you have,
this walk that leads to the river then circles back.
The turning of your blood a yoke in me,
the near memory of this place, the hook and talk of the sea.

The Poet's House

The dog lopes up ahead,
stops every second bush,
at the burgeoning heather

lifts his leg even though
we've been walking so long
it seems he has nothing left.

And we are circling
around the far fields
afraid of turning in,

the path to your cottage
something we pass, time
and again, as if entering that house

will be the one thing we ever do.
As if it will change us.
The dog and I

know better. But if this
is the last taste of the commonplace
bramble and gorse,

the tangle of yellow buds
becoming caught birds
in brown nests of calyx,

the soft ripple of their wings
like fur under my hand
when the dog comes to stand beside me —

then at least let's raise it up,
watch it take leave
like a thousand everydays lifting

or open it like a door
we think nothing
of entering.

Raising A Glass In A Field Near Galway

Back into the march grass and mud, the four of us go,
pint glasses in hand, searching for the one glass gone missing,
the one nursed like a child these two miles from Spiddal,
conveyed over rutted roads and trenches
past the "do not enter" plaque at the edge of the field,
though we trudged on anyway, like swimmers in the long grass,
folded into the accordion of its limbs.

Nearby sheep settle into the warmth of their fleece,
and the bull we reeled by eyes us
from behind the barbed wire of his fence.
Sudden grace, or lack thereof, that we found the glass
after ten minutes, the three of you having gone down
on hands and knees, genuflecting in the direction of the town.

But what does it matter? Hourglass or bathysphere,
telescope or jar, we raise it to the night's throat,
we drink the morning. Treble of bullrush and moor-grass
on our tongues, we carry on walking.
Cut through the field like one body, content to tread until dawn.

ACKNOWLEDGEMENTS

Some of the poems in this collection have appeared in the following journals: *The Antigonish Review*, *Event*, *The Fiddlehead*, *Grain*, *The Malahat Review*, *The New Quarterly*, *Prairie Fire*, *Poetry Ireland Review*, *Poetry New Zealand*, *Stinging Fly* (Ireland), *Stand* (UK), *The Inner Harbour Review*, *Susurrus*, *Front Magazine* and in the Sono Nis anthology *Breaking the Surface*. I am grateful to the editors of those publications for first presenting my work.

The British Columbia Arts Council and the Fellowship committees at the University of British Columbia helped make this book possible.

For their invaluable insights and for sharing their love of the craft I am indebted to Lorna Crozier and Patrick Lane. Thanks also to my wonderful editor Lynn Henry, to Michelle Benjamin, Leilah Nadir and to all the good folk at Polestar/Raincoast.

Thanks to Derk Wynand, George McWhirter, Billeh Nickerson and Heather MacLeod for help with the early drafts of some of these poems.

Thanks also to my family, to Carolyn Swayze, Kerry Ohana, Angela McGoldrick, and Brian Hunter; to Tom Landa and Jenise Boland for their humour and warmth; and thanks to my husband Glenn, first reader, first editor and the finest person I know.

The quote by Michael Ondaatje on page 6 is from the poem "These Back Alleys" in *Secular Love* (Coach House, 1984). The quote by Seamus Heaney on page 6 is from the poem "The Loose Box" in *Electric Light* (Faber and Faber, 2001). The quote by Eavan Boland on page 11 is from the poem "Unheroic" in *The Lost Land* (WW Norton and Co., 1998). The quote by Robert Hass on page 51 is from a poem in the *Anthology of Modern American Poetry* (Oxford University Press, 2001). The quote by Anne Michaels on page 67 is from the poem "Lake of Two Rivers" in *The Weight of Oranges* (McClelland and Stewart, 1986).

The title of the poem "Upon All the Living and the Dead" is a line from James Joyce's short story "The Dead."
"Vision of My Mother as Saint Catherine" was inspired by a poem of Paula Meehan's on Saint Francis.
"We Sailed From the Harbour of Leith" is derived from a letter written by James Laidlaw (my great-great-great-great-great grandfather) to William Laidlaw. I am indebted to Howard Anderson for this and other documents.

"After the Irish Republican Releases" is for Brian Hunter.
"Climbing Lessons" is for Joseph Robertson.
"The Panchen Lama" is about Gedhun Choekyi Nyima. The poem is for Patrick Lane.
"Raising A Glass in a Field Near Galway" is for Tom Landa and Jenise Boland.

ABOUT THE AUTHOR

Aislinn Hunter was born in Belleville, Ontario and moved to Dublin, Ireland for a few years before making her home in British Columbia. She received a BFA from the University of Victoria and an MFA from the University of British Columbia. She has published her poetry widely in literary journals in Canada and abroad, and is also the author of a much-praised book of fiction, *What's Left Us* (Polestar, 2001). She lives in Vancouver, British Columbia with her husband and their dog Fiddler.

Into the Early Hours was designed by Val Speidel and typeset in 11.5 pt Adobe Jenson on a 17 pt leading. Robert Slimbach's Adobe Jenson MM was issued in 1995 and is based on a type design by Nicholas Jenson (c. 1420–1480), a French punch-cutter and printer who worked in Venice. Jenson's punches have vanished, but his type has often been copied from his printed books.

Bright Lights *from* Polestar Book Publishers

Polestar takes pride in creating books that enrich our understanding of the world, and in introducing superb writers to discriminating readers.

Fiction:

What's Left Us • by Aislinn Hunter
Six stories and an unforgettable novella by a prodigiously talented writer. "Aislinn Hunter is a gifted writer with a fresh energetic voice and a sharp eye for the detail that draws you irresistibly into the intimacies of her story." — Jack Hodgins
1-55192-412-9 • $21.95 CAN/$15.95

Daughters are Forever • by Lee Maracle
Maracle's new novel reinforces her status as one of the most important First Nations writers. A moving story about First Nations people in the modern world and the importance of courage, truth and reconciliation.
1-55192-410-2 • $21.95 CAN/$16.95 USA

diss/ed banded nation • by David Nandi Odhiambo
"Thoroughly convincing in its evocation of young, rebellious, impoverished urban lives … an immersion into a simmering stew of racial and cultural identities …"
— *The Globe and Mail*   1-896095-26-7 • $16.95 CAN/$13.95 USA

Pool-Hopping and Other Stories • by Anne Fleming
Shortlisted for the Governor-General's Award, the Ethel Wilson Fiction Prize and the Danuta Gleed Award. "Fleming's evenhanded, sharp-eyed and often hilarious narratives traverse the frenzied chaos of urban life with ease and precision."
— *The Georgia Straight*   1-896095-18-6 • $16.95 CAN/$13.95 USA

Poetry:

Blue • by George Elliott Clarke
Blue is black, profane, surly, damning, and unrelenting in its brilliance. George Elliott Clarke has written urgent and necessary poems about the experience of being black in North America.   1-55192-414-5 • $18.95 CAN/$13.95 USA

The Predicament of Or • by Shani Mootoo
The author of the acclaimed novel *Cereus Blooms at Night* turns her hand to poetry in a lively and nuanced exploration of desire, identity and personal exile.
1-55192-416-1 0 $18.95 CAN/$13.95 USA